Hunger
Geoff Barker

Smart Apple Media

Titles in the Voices series:

AIDS • Child Labor • Drugs on the Street • Gangs

Hunger • Poverty • Racism • Religious Extremism

Violence • Violence on the Screen • War

Smart Apple Media
P.O. Box 3263, Mankato, Minnesota 56002

U.S. publication copyright © 2010 Smart Apple Media. International copyright reserved in all countries. No part of this book may be reproduced in any form without written permission from the publisher.

This book has been published in cooperation with Evans Publishing Group.

Copyright © 2009 Evans Brothers Ltd

Printed in China

Library of Congress Cataloging-in-Publication Data
Barker, Geoff.
 Hunger / by Geoff Barker.
  p. cm. -- (Voices)
 Includes index.
 ISBN 978-1-59920-281-5 (hardcover)
 1. Famines--Juvenile literature. 2. Food relief--Juvenile literature. I. Title.
 HV630.B37 2010
 363.8--dc22
                                2008050430

Editor: Susie Brooks
Designer: Mayer Media Ltd
Picture research: Susie Brooks and Lynda Lines
Graphs and charts: Martin Darlison, Encompass Graphics

Picture acknowledgements
Photographs were kindly supplied by the following:
Corbis 6 (Karen Kasmauski), 28 (Alessandra Benedetti); Getty Images front cover, 15 (Time & Life Pictures), 16 (AFP), 17, 18, 20, 23 (AFP), 25 (AFP), 29, 31, 32, 35, 40, 42–43; PA Photos 39 (Ariana Cubillos/AP); Panos 7 (Piers Benatar), 11 (J B Russell), 12–13 (Sven Torfinn), 19 (Dieter Telemans), 24 (Aubrey Wade), 27 (Robin Hammond), 30 (Jenny Matthews), 34–35 (Sven Torfinn), 37 (George Georgiou), 41 (Giacomo Pirozzi), 45 (Jenny Matthews); Photolibrary.com 8 (The Irish Image Collection), 26 (Caroline Penn); Reuters 1 (Peter Andrews), 9 (Peter Andrews); Still Pictures 22 (Joerg Boethling), 36 (H Baesemann).

Cover picture: A young girl asks for food in a refugee camp in Afghanistan.

9 8 7 6 5 4 3 2 1

CONTENTS

What Is Hunger?	6
Why Do Famines Happen?	8
What Is Extreme Hunger Like?	10
How Aware Are We of the Hungry?	12
Does Hunger Affect Only Poor Countries?	14
Can't Hungry People Help Themselves?	16
Are Weak and Corrupt Governments at Fault?	18
Can We Feed the World?	20
Can GM Crops Solve World Hunger?	22
Does Fair Trade Help?	24
Can Charities Make a Real Difference?	26
Do Events like Live 8 Help?	28
Are We Tired of Giving?	30
Are Wealthy Countries Doing All They Can?	32
Who's to Blame When Food Rations Don't Come?	34
Should We Feel Guilty about Wasting Food?	36
Can Food Prices Create a Food Crisis?	38
Food Aid Forever?	40
Time Line	42
Glossary	44
Resources	45
Index	46

WHAT IS HUNGER?

You've probably felt hungry before. But have you ever felt real hunger? Imagine a day without getting enough food. Now imagine another day, then another.

With supermarket shelves stacked with food, shoppers in the United States and other wealthy countries can pick and choose what to eat.

Rarely Hungry
In the wealthy countries of the developed world, stores and restaurants offer a huge choice of food. Many people become overweight, even obese, due to overeating. Mary from Philadelphia is trying to diet. She explains how cutting down on food makes her feel:

"I'm starving! I'm on day two of my diet right now . . . This is tough. I was watching TV and all the commercials showing burgers and pizzas . . . Right now I'm hungry and I've had a headache all day. Haven't felt too weak yet . . ."

"Hunger and malnutrition are the underlying cause of more than half of all child deaths, killing nearly 6 million children each year."
United Nations Food and Agriculture Organization (FAO)

Really Hungry

For millions of people in the developing world, hunger is not just a pain that will go away, it is a matter of life and death. People suffering from real hunger do not get the food they need to be healthy and active. Khuda is a poor farmer from central Afghanistan whose family often goes hungry:

❝ We don't eat three times a day because we don't have enough food. Often we eat either in the morning or at midday and then eat again the next day. We eat whatever is available; sometimes only a piece of bread with water. ❞

Hunger is a real fact of life for this Afghan woman from Kangri village. Her meal consists of just a bowl of grass, which she boils to eat.

HUNGRY WORLD

- Hunger affects 862 million people around the world—one in seven of the total population.
- 820 million of the hungry live in developing countries.

United Nations Food and Agriculture Organization, 2006

WHY DO FAMINES HAPPEN?

When a region suffers severe food shortages, we say there is a famine. Throughout history there have been many terrible famines. Why do they happen?

The Great Hunger

From 1845 to 1849, a failure of potato crops caused famine in Ireland. The Great Hunger, or Irish Potato Famine, left huge numbers of people without their staple food. About 1 million Irish people died of starvation and related diseases. Naomh Flynn, who was 12 years old at the time, wrote this:

" We have no potatoes to eat because of the blight [a plant disease] . . . I dreamed of boiled potatoes in the night, and awoke hungry and empty. Father's cheeks are sunken . . . We pray but wait in vain for any help . . . Father says we shall have to leave and start a new life in America . . . "

IRISH LOSSES

Irish population as recorded by the census in 1841 and 1851:

1841: 8 million

1851: 6.5 million

It is thought that about half a million people moved to Great Britain, North America, and Australia during the famine.

This memorial in Dublin, Ireland remembers the victims of the Irish Potato Famine.

Famine regularly affects Ethiopia in eastern Africa. Drought conditions parch the land and cattle begin to die first.

Today's Famines

Famines are still a problem in many parts of the world today. They may be caused by a number of factors, including war, poor government, and natural disasters such as droughts or flooding. In the Ogaden region of Ethiopia, failing rains and rising food prices have left millions of people struggling to grow or buy food. Assefa, age 15, is worried that time is running out for her and her family:

" We have almost no food now. We lost Gabra my sister four nights ago. She died of diarrhea. The only food we have is donated wheat, and a little oil. But we need milk too. We are all hungry. Mother is scared that we will die as well. "

"Today we have the worst crisis in the Horn of Africa in decades. There are about two million Ethiopians now at the risk of famine. Their situation is getting near desperate and will get much, much worse as the months go on and the dry season starts."

Dan Toole, Director of Emergency Programs, UNICEF, 2008

WHAT IS EXTREME HUNGER LIKE?

Severe hunger can take many forms, from lacking the right type of food to barely getting any food at all. How do different types of hunger feel?

Weak from Malnutrition

Daily malnutrition is the most common type of hunger. It affects people who don't get enough nutrients, such as protein, vitamins, and minerals in their food. Their bodies may not grow properly and they become weak and unable to fight disease. Nine-year-old Zula, from Eritrea in Africa, knows how this feels:

" My sister wanted me to play with her: 'Skip rope with me and Sadaf.' I just wanted to lie down. My head hurts and my stomach's empty. I can't go back to school yet. My mother says she's worried about me when I spend all my time in bed. **"**

Industrialized Countries (100,000)
Central/Eastern Europe and Russian Federation (100,000)
Latin America and Caribbean (300,000)
Middle East and North Africa (400,000)
East Asia and Pacific (900,000)
Sub-Saharan Africa (4.8 million)
South Asia (3.1 million)

HUNGER IN ERITREA

Eritrea has one of the highest percentages of undernourished people:

Total population: 4,000,000
Total undernourished: 2,900,000
% of total population: 72%

World Food Program (WFP)

This pie chart shows the number of child deaths around the world in 2007. More than half of all child deaths are linked to malnutrition.
UNICEF, "State of the World's Children," 2008

"It's not because these families can't feed their children. There is enough food and most parents can afford that. Indeed, they feed the children rice and milk. But lack of a balanced diet is causing this problem."

Nursing inspector at the Mahendranagar hospital in Nepal, describing the causes of local malnutrition, 2006

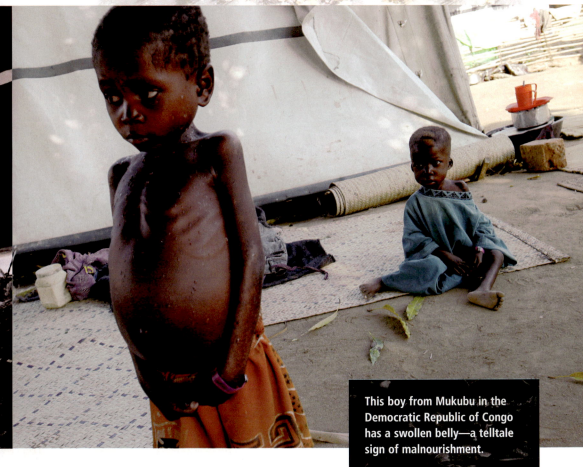

This boy from Mukubu in the Democratic Republic of Congo has a swollen belly—a telltale sign of malnourishment.

Starving and Scared

Famines can cause extreme starvation on a large scale. Starvation happens when there is simply not enough food to eat. People can survive for weeks without food, but eventually they will die. The threat of extreme hunger and starvation is a terrifying experience, as this North Korean teenager explains:

❝ We have to find food in the country like berries, but sometimes you can only get roots and grasses. My father is good at finding food. He remembers how things were . . . [the North Korean famine of 1995–1997]. He says a lot of people died then. Lots of his friends. Food is short again. We do not know when we will eat again. We are starving. ❞

HOW AWARE ARE WE OF THE HUNGRY?

We rely on the media, such as newspapers, TV, and radio, to keep us up-to-date on what is happening around the world. Do we get a true picture, or are there hidden tales of hunger?

What's News?

When an emergency such as a war or natural disaster happens, there is certainly plenty of press coverage. But how quickly do events like this become old news? In the Darfur region of western Sudan, people have been suffering from conflict for many years. Fatimah, a 16-year-old Sudanese girl, wants more awareness of her country's difficulties:

❝ People outside Darfur may not want to know what is happening here. It is good that you journalists talk to us but does anyone listen? And if there's more interesting news somewhere else in the world, everyone forgets about us again. It is true what we say . . . we need help like money and food from other countries right now . . . but our country also needs peace. ❞

"In nearly 40 years of traveling the world, I have not witnessed any crisis [like Darfur] that so vividly combines the worst of everything—armed conflict; acts of extreme violence; great tides of desperate refugees; hunger and disease combined with an unforgiving desert climate."

Martin Bell, UNICEF ambassador for humanitarian emergencies, 2004

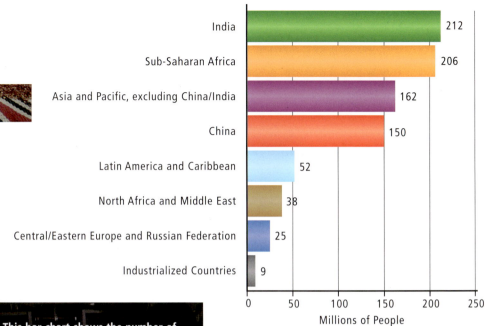

This bar chart shows the number of hungry people around the world. More than 400 million are from India and sub-Saharan Africa.
United Nations Food and Agriculture Organization (FAO), 2006

Silent Stories

The media tends to ignore the day-to-day, smaller stories of starvation. Even a deadly famine may go unreported if a story closer to home creates more interest. Ramesh Joshi, age 18, lives in a small village in the Orissa region of India. He is one of many thousands of hungry people whose suffering never makes headline news:

❝ Sometimes one of us can find some work, but most of the time we cannot. The rice we are given only lasts us ten days. We have to beg to eat for the rest of the month. How long can we carry on like this? One day we will die of starvation. There are lots of people like our family in this village. ❞

In a refugee camp in Gereida, southern Sudan, this Darfur family survives on rations provided by the United Nations World Food Program.

DOES HUNGER AFFECT ONLY POOR COUNTRIES?

Poverty, or being poor, lies at the very heart of hunger. Without money, people cannot afford to buy food. But is hunger a problem only in the poorest nations?

Poor and Vulnerable

The world's poorest regions face the highest risk of hunger and famine. Disasters hit them hard because they don't have the resources to provide for emergency needs. Schooling is often poor, and well-paid work hard to find. Isis, a seven-year-old in rural Egypt, tells a story that many others share:

> **We didn't have much to eat yesterday. In the evening we asked if there was any food. Mother told us the rice was cooking . . . and we fell asleep. I hope my father can find work today so we can eat something.**

- Herders, fishers, forest-dependent people (10%)
- Urban poor (20%)
- Small farmers (50%)
- Rural landless (20%)

This pie chart shows how the world's hungry are divided. The majority are living off the land in the countryside, which is true of large numbers of people in poor countries.
United Nations Food and Agriculture Organization (FAO), 2006

"Hunger is a symptom of failure—failed harvests, failure to cope with natural disasters, and failure to overcome social inequities, ethnic strife, and racial hatred."
James Morris, Executive Director of the World Food Program, 2005

This Kids' Café in Missouri helps to make sure poor, underfed children can get a hot meal.

Hungry in the United States

The United States is one of the richest nations in the world, but this does not mean it has no hungry people. One in six children there lives in poverty, unsure of where the next meal is coming from. Many families struggle every day to find money to buy enough food. George, age 13, recently found out how this feels:

❝ Mom lost her job after Christmas . . . Last week it was so cold at home. I said I was freezing and she shouted at me: 'Put the heater on then—you can have food on the table or the heater on!' Tami said we could always go to the Kids' Café for a free meal—the people are really nice there. ❞

POVERTY AND HUNGER IN THE UNITED STATES

In 2006:

- Nearly 37 million Americans (12.3%) were living in poverty.
- 12.8 million children (17.4%) under the age of 18 were in poverty.
- 35.5 million were lacking sufficient food, including 12.6 million children.
- America's Second Harvest organization provided emergency food assistance to about 4.5 million different people every week.

Feeding America (formerly America's Second Harvest)

CAN'T HUNGRY PEOPLE HELP THEMSELVES?

Who is to blame when people go hungry? Are they just unlucky, living in difficult circumstances, or should they try harder to find food?

This elderly woman in Granichi, Belarus, works hard on the land so that she does not go hungry.

Work Harder

Some people think that the poor and hungry should make more effort to fend for themselves. Victor is a teenager living Zaragoza in Spain. He is used to a comfortable lifestyle but believes that this comes from hard work:

❝ My father has never had a day off sick in his life. You have to work hard to get where you want. You shouldn't get it handed to you on a plate. This may sound a bit harsh, but I think it's true. Perhaps some of these [hungry] people are relying on our help too much. ❞

Hungry and Helpless

People can become stuck in a cycle of hunger and poverty. Because they are hungry, they grow weak. Because they are weak, they struggle to work or produce food. Many, like 12-year-old Nadif in Somalia, simply lack chances to improve their lives. He describes his family's helplessness in difficult times:

❝ If the . . . rains fail this year, I don't know what we will do. We all had to leave Mogadishu [the capital city] because of violence on the streets. Our home is now a plastic sheet under a tree by the road . . . we have to line up every day to get some corn, beans, and oil. ❞

"Chronic hunger occurs because people lack opportunity—to earn enough money, to be educated and gain skills, to meet basic health needs, and to have a voice in the decisions that affect their communities."

Joan Holmes, President of The Hunger Project charitable organization

In 2006, this Somali woman lost 40 cattle due to drought. She has only a makeshift shelter and three goats.

ARE WEAK AND CORRUPT GOVERNMENTS AT FAULT?

In some parts of the world, bad governments make people's lives very difficult. Are weak and corrupt governments responsible for high hunger levels?

No Protection

Governments should provide an infrastructure, including education, transportation, and health care that supports farmers and other workers. But sometimes country leaders are more interested in spending money on themselves. Dembe, age 12, lives in Uganda where she feels the government is neglecting people's needs:

"My mother and I go out every day to pick wild leaves to eat, but we still rely on food aid. We don't want to have to keep on asking for help from other countries every year. Our government should be doing more to look after us. My mother and father need jobs so we can all eat."

UGANDA IN FIGURES

- Uganda has debts of $540 million.
- 1 in 3 Ugandans survive on less than a dollar a day.
- In 2007, Ugandan president Yoweri Museveni caused outrage by his plans to upgrade his $21 million jet plane with a new $32 million jet.
- It cost a reported $36 million to refurbish Museveni's presidential palace.

"No substantial famine has ever occurred in a country with a democratic form of government and a relatively free press."

Professor Amartya Sen, Indian economist and philosopher

For most people in Uganda, the lavish presidential palace in the capital city of Entebbe is a world away.

Floods like these in Bangladesh, 2004, wreck water supplies as well as homes and crops. Coping with millions of displaced, hungry people is a huge challenge for any government.

Difficult Circumstances

Some causes of hunger are difficult for governments to control. There is little they can do, for example, to prevent extreme weather that may dry out or flood people's land. Having survived numerous floods, Ruhanna Ali, from Bangladesh, realizes that her country is in a vulnerable position:

❝ Our country has many floods, and we have had floods again this year. It was the monsoon. We managed to save ourselves, but couldn't take anything with us. We lost two goats and three chickens. We need to eat but there is no work because of the flooding. We have to wait until the waters drop. We hope our government can bring us food. ❞

CAN WE FEED THE WORLD?

There are nearly 7 billion people living in the world—and 200,000 more are added to the population every day. Are there enough resources to feed us all?

A hungry girl begs for food outside a restaurant in Lhasa, Tibet. Around half of all Tibetan children suffer from stunted growth and other health problems due to malnutrition.

Losing Land

Many people say that the world is overpopulated already. If we can't feed everyone now, how can we hope to in the future? For 17-year-old Matt from Sydney, Australia, hunger will remain a global problem because less land is available for growing crops:

“ There are well over 6 billion people in the world, and the population's just going up and up . . . You cannot grow crops in huge areas of the world . . . Climate change is making things worse . . . and lots of good crop-growing regions [in Australia] have had to deal with a drought for five years now . . . ”

Plenty of Food

Others believe that the world has more than enough resources to feed everyone. The problem is they are not used or distributed evenly. People in wealthy countries consume and demand far more than those in poor regions of the world. Serge, 16, from Montreal in Canada, thinks that greed is an issue:

" There is enough food to feed the world, no doubt about it. Apart from the obvious imbalance between what rich and poor nations need ... the problem is our love of eating so much meat. We grow all this food to feed cattle so we can kill them and eat them. If we all ate less meat, or more people cut it out of their diet completely, we could save good land for growing crops for people, not animals. "

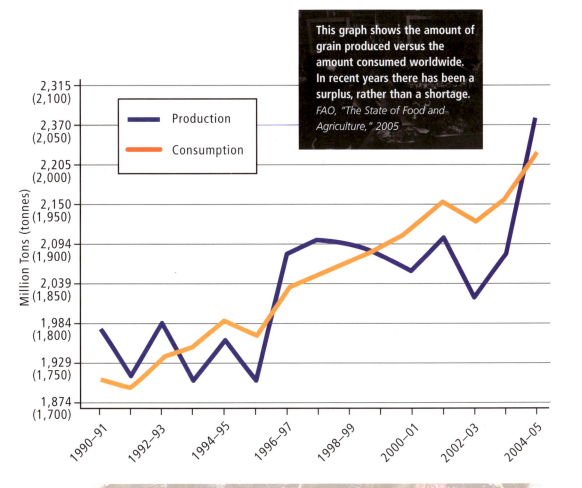

This graph shows the amount of grain produced versus the amount consumed worldwide. In recent years there has been a surplus, rather than a shortage.
FAO, "The State of Food and Agriculture," 2005

" More than half the grain grown in the United States ... is fed to livestock, grain that would feed far more people than would the livestock to which it is fed."
Richard H. Robbins, American anthropologist (from "Readings on Poverty, Hunger, and Economic Development")

CAN GM CROPS SOLVE WORLD HUNGER?

In recent years, scientists have been experimenting with altering the natural makeup of crops to make them more productive. These genetically modified (GM) crops have sparked fierce debates. Can they solve the hunger problem?

Super-Crops

GM crops could help to feed more mouths. Scientists are developing types that will grow, for example, in dry areas where other crops fail. Some GM crops may have nutrients added to protect against malnutrition. Isagani lives in the Philippines, where her father is testing golden rice enriched with vitamin A:

❝ These [GM] food crops can be good for our country in the future. They can grow better and stronger. My father says that golden rice will feed us . . . and help to stop many children going blind. Lots of Filipino children are going blind [due to lack of vitamin A]. ❞

VITAMIN A DEFICIENCY

- Vitamin A deficiency (VAD) affects 120 million people in the developing world.
- Long-term effects include measles, diarrhea, pneumonia, and blindness.
- Every day 17 Filipino children go blind due to vitamin A deficiency.

UNICEF, Global AIDS Alliance, 2007

"I think there is little doubt that GM has real potential for increasing food production in a friendly way, though clearly we need some fairly serious controls."
Professor John Beddington, chief scientist to the UK Government, 2007

A scientist tests samples of GM rice in a laboratory in the Philippines. Genetically modifying rice could boost the nutritional value and yields of this important food crop.

"Assessment of the [GM] technology lags behind its development, information is anecdotal [unreliable] and contradictory, and uncertainty about possible benefits and damage is unavoidable."
International Assessment of Agricultural Science and Technology for Development [IAASTD], 2008

Indian farmers protest in New Delhi in May 2008 against the use of GM food crops due to health fears.

A Dangerous Experiment

Many people feel that meddling with nature is a dangerous game and that GM crops have not been sufficiently tested. They fear that the crops could harm both the environment and human health. Many also argue that most of the companies developing GM foods are based in rich countries and care more about making money than feeding the hungry. Pascal from France says:

❝ When we have proper, scientifically tested GM crops in a controlled environment (where nothing gets out and no external influences get in), then I will gladly accept the conclusions. Until then, GM crops are nothing but a nice excuse to sell expensive seed to poor people who can barely afford it. That is not what I call working to feed the global population. ❞

DOES FAIR TRADE HELP?

Fair trade organizations work directly with small-scale farmers. They provide the growers with a stable price for crops—plus a bit extra to help with community projects. Do small farmers benefit from fair trade?

Fair Gains

Fair trade systems can improve life for many people. They give farmers the chance to work their own land and earn a reliable income. They also offer other benefits such as new schools, health care, and water supplies. Mary, from Ghana in Africa, feels she has gained a lot from fair trade:

❝ Fair trade is a good thing. Things you take for granted [in Western countries] may be hard to come by in Ghana. Fair trade is good to the farmer and makes us happy. We would like to sell more cocoa to fair trade so more farmers can taste a better life. ❞

ON THE RISE

- Worldwide, consumers spent over $2 billion on fair trade certified products in 2007, an increase of 47% on the previous year.
- The money directly benefited over 7 million people, including farmers, workers, and families in 58 developing countries.
- There are now over 3,000 fair trade products, including the big sellers—coffee, tea, chocolate, and bananas.

The Fairtrade Foundation

This cocoa farmer from Kuapo Kokoo, Ghana, is one of 45,000 members of a fair trade cooperative that shares profits from a UK chocolate company.

Pakistani farmers harvest their wheat on the outskirts of Islamabad. Using traditional tools, the work is slow and farmers include many children.

Fair Restrains

Some people feel that fair trade holds farmers back. It keeps them working on a small scale, rather than encouraging them to use modern methods. Being free to compete on the open market may help farmers to think bigger and eventually earn more. Gulshan, in Pakistan, believes that technology is the answer for small farmers:

> It is still backbreaking work for most of our family. We get a fair price for our dried fruit and nuts, so it is better than the old days when they used to cheat my family at market. But we can only harvest so much. Really we need machines to help us.

> "At best, fair trade is a marketing device that does the poor little good. At worst, it may inadvertently [accidentally] be harming some of the planet's most vulnerable people. If we really want to aid international development, we should instead work to abolish barriers to trade in the rich world, and help the developing world to do the same."
> Tom Clougherty, Policy Director at Adam Smith Institute, 2008

CAN CHARITIES MAKE A REAL DIFFERENCE?

Many charities and nongovernmental organizations (NGOs) offer help to people suffering from hunger. Some supply countries with emergency provisions after a disaster. But can charities really help defeat hunger?

Saving and Improving Lives

Charity food and water supplies do a lot to keep people alive in the aftermath of a disaster. Charities can also try to fight hunger in the longer term. Zahir owns a small farm in Bangladesh. He has seen charities and NGOs change his life:

" In the past we depended on monsoon rains for rice and other cereals. Foreign charities and local NGOs have helped us develop and use seeds that give us crops in the dry season too. We get the crop seeds free . . . and return twice as many seeds to the (community) centers. "

An expert member of VSO (Voluntary Service Overseas) teaches planting methods to schoolchildren in Kanchanaburi, Thailand.

> "The fight against hunger is not an issue of charity; it is an issue of justice."
> Jacques Diouf, Director-General of the UN Food and Agriculture Organization, 1997

Crisis in Zimbabwe's economy meant that a bread roll cost one billion Zimbabwean dollars (about 100 U.S. dollars) in June 2008. Economic problems like this are largely beyond charitable help.

Not a Solution

Sometimes people don't want charity—they say that they could help themselves if only they were given the chance. Many poor families live in countries that could invest more in agriculture, as well as in infrastructure such as factories, roads, and schools. Tenny, a 19-year-old in Zimbabwe, feels that charity is not helping his country's cause:

> **People have forgotten about us here in Zimbabwe. [President] Mugabe has forgotten about us too. We are relying on the food aid . . . but I do not think this gets to the root of the problem. Zimbabwe is in a mess now. In Harare we are scared and we are dying of diseases. Some people are saying we need peacekeepers here. But we all know the government needs to spend money to build up our country again.**

DO EVENTS LIKE LIVE 8 HELP?

Since the original Live Aid concert in 1985, top musicians have staged several major events to raise money for the world's poor and hungry. Live 8, in July 2005, raised awareness. Do efforts like this really help?

Help for the Hungry

Benefit concerts get people talking about the main issues. Live 8 put pressure on wealthy countries to increase aid for the hungry in the developing world. It also fought to drop the debts owed by the poorest nations to the richest. Tom, 16, from Edinburgh in Scotland, thought the concerts were a success:

" We were all watching Live 8, it was awesome. The concerts raised awareness about poverty, hunger, Africa . . . It wasn't about raising money, it was about cancelling Third World debts . . . Live Aid raised something like $200 million and that helped feed the starving millions. Live 8 was different though. "

Live 8 organizer Bob Geldof holds a news conference to promote the aims of the concerts in July 2005.

"If we come out of [Live 8] having achieved something for the weakest, voiceless, most put-upon people in the planet, that would not be a bad use of political influence."
Bob Geldof, former singer of The Boomtown Rats, organizer of Live 8, 2005

"To think you can lift a continent out of poverty with aid is nonsense. The future of Africa is not going to be decided by rock concerts, but by African politicians making good decisions."
Richard Dowden, Director of the Royal African Society, 2005

Crowds gather in Rome for one of the many international Live 8 concerts. Some people criticized Live 8 for the lack of African singers involved.

Is it Really for Africa?

Most people agree that raising awareness about poverty and hunger is a good thing. But do some people end up forgetting the reason for holding these concerts in the first place? Jean-Claude Shanda Tonme, from Cameroon, Africa, thinks that sometimes the musicians and stars of the show ignore the real problems:

❝ The truth is that it was not for us, for Africa, that the musicians at Live 8 were singing; it was to amuse the crowds and to clear their own consciences ... They still believe us to be like children that they must save, as if we don't realize ourselves what the source of our problems is ... We didn't hear anyone at Live 8 raise a cry for democracy [fair government] in Africa. ❞

ARE WE TIRED OF GIVING?

News reports and charity appeals often show shocking images of children wasting away from hunger. It's hard to see people who suffer on a daily basis. Can we ever get fed up of giving money to charity?

Feeling Hopeless

Daily hunger is a desperate situation that most of us are lucky enough not to experience. If we keep seeing pictures and films of starving people, do we start to switch off? Do we ignore the issue and assume that someone else is going to help? David, a French teenager, thinks that people can become immune to what they see:

❝ Sometimes you see the same images of hunger and starvation on the TV, and you are not touched by them. Perhaps you have seen this so many times that you have stopped feeling. Maybe you don't want to see this. ❞

A 21-month-old child in Niger recovers from severe malnutrition at a feeding center run by Médecins Sans Frontières (Doctors without Borders).

"Reducing hunger and malnutrition is the forgotten Millennium Development Goal and hunger contributes to a staggering 3.5 million child deaths each year. [We need] . . . a wider global effort to put these issues at the very top of the international agenda."

Jasmine Whitbread, Chief Executive of Save the Children

Giving Hope

Many people argue that awareness is a key factor in solving the world's problems. They feel strongly that spreading the word about people's suffering is the best way to spur others on to help. Frances Seth, a volunteer for Save the Children, will never tire of promoting her charity's cause. She saw the results of successful appeals and donations when she helped at a clinic in southern Niger in 2008:

❝ One of the very first things I saw was a very sick little baby . . . I asked one of the staff, 'How do you cope with this every day?' He said that these were the lucky ones — these children are now getting help because we're here . . . we are making that difference. ❞

Hundreds of people march in the streets of San Salvador during a World Food Program "Walk the World" event to fight child hunger in El Salvador.

ARE WEALTHY COUNTRIES DOING ALL THEY CAN?

Wealthy countries have enough money and resources to be able to help developing nations. Could they be doing more for their poor and hungry neighbors?

Always There

The developed world provides a huge amount of aid to less developed countries. Individuals and businesses donate to many worthy charities and NGOs, and organizations like the World Food Program respond quickly to feed people in emergencies. When the tsunami of December 2004 struck Aceh Province in Indonesia, 13-year-old Salim was one of the few who survived. The foreign aid he received saved his life.

> **We'd been eating nothing but noodles for ten days after the tsunami. AusAID helped us. They came in boats and brought us food like rice, sugar, biscuits. They brought us medicines and water too . . . we had nothing—they've saved our lives.**

Aid supplies reach Indonesia in December 2004 to help surviving victims of the devastating Indian Ocean tsunami.

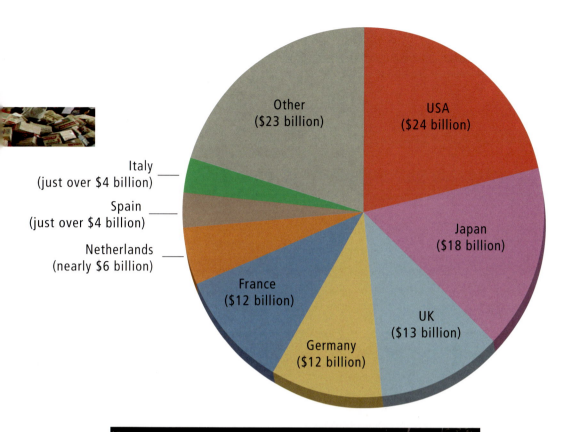

This pie chart shows the billions of dollars (in U.S. dollars) that wealthy countries spent on aid to poorer nations in 2006.
Organization for Economic Co-operation and Development (OECD)

More to Do

Many people point out that despite the billions spent on aid, hunger in the developing world has not diminished. They say that developed countries need to focus more on the root causes of hunger. This means tackling issues such as international trade and finding solutions to poverty. For Joseph from New Jersey, education and empowerment are vital:

" Give a man a fish and he eats for a day. Teach a man to fish and he eats for a lifetime. It's an old saying but a valid one. The problem of global poverty will never be solved with foreign aid, at least not by itself. **"**

"With the record of corruption within impoverished countries, people will question giving them money. That can be handled by giving them the industry directly, not the money."
J. W. Smith, *Economic Democracy: The Political Struggle for the 21st Century*, Second Edition, 2002

WHO'S TO BLAME WHEN FOOD RATIONS DON'T COME?

Food rations supplied by foreign aid agencies can save lives in war-torn regions or after an emergency such as flooding. But sometimes the food doesn't reach the hungry mouths. When this happens, who is at fault?

Hazardous Journeys

During an emergency, food aid convoys face many hazards. Bad weather and flooding, or difficult terrain, can grind them to a halt. Local gangs may ambush or attack the vehicles to profit from the precious supplies themselves. Abaqala, a 13-year-old orphan living in a refugee camp in Sudan, knows that her lifeline could be disrupted at any time:

❝ Nothing will improve here until we have peace in our country. The aid workers tell us that the food trucks cannot even get through sometimes. The food relief we do get is keeping us alive—we really need it during the rainy season now. ❞

Aid trucks try to reach some of the thousands of refugees who have fled from Sudan to neighboring Chad in 2004. Flooded rivers often hamper relief work.

Keep Out!

Sometimes aid arrives intact, but is rejected by the country that needs it. In 2008, the Asian nation of Myanmar (Burma) suffered terrible flooding after a cyclone. Aid was quickly flown in, but the Burmese authorities refused to distribute it to the people. They seemed fearful that foreign interference would threaten their position of power. Villagers like this one were desperate:

> **Most of our village got washed away. Some of us climbed to the top of our house to survive. But we need help now. Help me get food for this baby, she needs milk. People (foreign aid workers) want to help . . . but the government tells them to keep out.**

Eventually the aid was allowed through, but it was too late for tens of thousands of Burmese who died before help came.

Homeless Burmese cyclone victims beg for food, as aid begins to arrive a week after Cyclone Nargis in May 2008.

> "It has not been us who have been deaf and dumb in response to the pleas of the international community but the government in Myanmar. We have reached out, they have kept their hands in their pockets."
> Robert Gates, U.S. Defense Secretary, May 2008

SHOULD WE FEEL GUILTY ABOUT WASTING FOOD?

With so many food choices available in the developed world, is it surprising that a staggering amount gets wasted? And should we feel guilty about wasting food?

Not Guilty

In the Western world, we are spoiled with choice. We buy so much food every week that a large percentage gets thrown out untouched. Grocery stores also waste a vast amount of unsold food. Jed, 11, from Los Angeles, does not see a problem with wasting food:

❝ We probably buy more than we need sometimes—but why shouldn't we? It's our money. There's plenty of food in the stores. And what difference does it make if we eat it all or not? It's not as if we can send our leftovers to Africa. ❞

A bin full of bread and pastries is thrown out in Troms, Norway.

What a Waste

When so many people are starving in the world, is it fair to throw away food? Christine, from Cardiff in Wales, thinks that famine could be solved if we took more care to buy only the products we need:

" We make so much waste. We buy and throw away all the time, and yet we do not seem to want to share with the poor ... Why can't we make the connection between wasting food and food shortages? When children are dying of starvation in the world, how can we throw away food that's perfectly OK? "

These hungry garbage-pickers in Kolkata, India, are driven to eating filthy scraps from other people's waste.

WASTE IN THE U.S.

- In the U.S., up to a quarter of food goes to waste.
- Every year, an estimated 220 pounds (100 kg) of food per person ends up in landfills.
- This waste food has an annual value of over $30 billion.

U.S. Environmental Protection Agency

CAN FOOD PRICES CREATE A FOOD CRISIS?

Prices of staple foods have shot up recently. Reasons for this include competition with crops being grown for biofuel and the rising cost of fertilizers. Can leaps in food prices create a crisis around the world?

This graph shows price increases for staple foods from March 2007 to March 2008.

All That We Need

In the developed world, more and more people are budgeting due to higher food prices. Birgit, 11, from Germany has noticed that her mother is shopping more carefully in recent months. She is not too concerned about a food crisis though:

❝ When we go shopping now, Mom's saying we can't have this treat or that treat. I've noticed she's also shopping more at the cheap supermarkets. It's a bit embarrassing if any of your friends see you in there. But there's not a food crisis, is there? We can still buy whatever we want. ❞

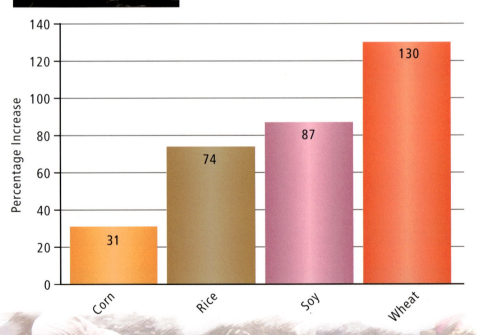

"While many are worrying about filling their gas tanks, many others around the world are struggling to fill their stomachs, and it is getting more and more difficult every day."

Robert B. Zoellick, World Bank President, 2008

"Food prices are increasingly a matter of life and death for children from poor families. Many families couldn't afford a nutritious diet even before prices went up. But a doubling or more of the price of staple foods will be a catastrophe, especially for children."

David Mepham, Save the Children UK's Director of Policy

Protesters demonstrate against rising food prices in Port-au-Prince, Haiti, in April 2008. Angry riots caused schools and businesses to close.

Desperate Times

For vast numbers of people in the developing world, the situation is much more desperate. In 2008, people from Ethiopia to Senegal and from Mexico to Haiti took to the streets to protest about food prices. Basic foods were just becoming too expensive for ordinary people to afford. In Les Cayes in Haiti, 16-year-old Jean witnessed violent riots:

❝ Yes, it was very scary at the time. They shut our school because it was close to the food demos. People were out in the streets because prices are going up all the time. Then someone started firing shots ... People are just tired of not being able to afford things like rice, beans, or fruit ... It's mad, no one can afford these prices any more. ❞

FOOD AID FOREVER?

Hunger is the number one risk to health in the world. With so many natural disasters and added pressures on food production these days, it will be difficult to eliminate hunger forever. Will poor, starving people always have to rely on food aid?

Coping with Crisis

There are now more extreme weather events—including flooding and droughts—than ever before. But charities and NGOs are quicker to take action and get help to those people affected. There will always be emergencies—and there will always have to be food aid. Nanda Dilshan, 16, from Thawalema village in Sri Lanka, believes that she owes her life to aid and development workers:

❝ Our home flooded about three years ago. We had nothing left. The whole village got washed away. But Red Cross workers helped us. First we got food rations. Then we got help building a new home and growing crops . . . we could then rebuild our lives. Charities keep saving lives. ❞

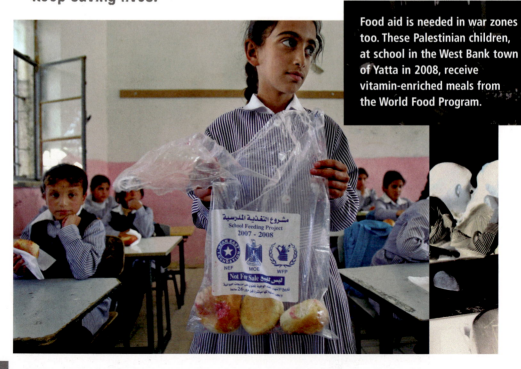

Food aid is needed in war zones too. These Palestinian children, at school in the West Bank town of Yatta in 2008, receive vitamin-enriched meals from the World Food Program.

Lasting Solutions

Aid agencies do a good job helping ordinary people recover from disaster. But hunger is likely to continue as the world's major health problem until developing countries are in a position to help their own people more. Countries need a reasonable economy and improved education to escape a cycle of poverty and hunger. Fatmira Sadiku is from Albania, one of Europe's poorest countries. She worries for her children, Kadri and Denisa, in difficult times:

> " I have been poor most of my life, but I can never remember not having bread to eat . . . I tell Kadri all the time as soon as Denisa turns 14 she needs to get married. At least she will have something to eat where she goes. Here she is starving. "

A health worker talks about the importance of breastfeeding and good nutrition at a mother and baby clinic in Mali. Programs like this can help to turn lives around.

"We need not only short-term emergency measures to meet urgent critical needs and avert starvation in many regions across the world but also a significant increase in long-term productivity in food grain production."
Ban Ki-moon, United Nations Secretary-General, 2008

TIME LINE

440 B.C. Famine strikes in Ancient Rome.

A.D. 400–800 Famine spreads over Western Europe. During this time, due to famine and plague, the population of Rome falls by 90 percent.

800–1000 Drought kills millions of Mayans in Central America. Famine starts the collapse of their civilization.

1315–1317 The Great Famine in Europe causes millions of deaths.

1601–1603 100,000 die in Moscow, Russia, due to famine. Half the population of Estonia also dies.

1693–1694 Famine in France kills 2 million people.

1702–1704 Famine in Deccan, India, kills 2 million people.

1727–1728 Famine causes widespread problems in England.

1845–1849 The Irish Potato Famine (or "Great Hunger") causes 1 million or more Irish to die.

1850–1873 During the Taiping Rebellion, drought and famine cause a drop in the Chinese population of 60 million.

1866–1868 The Finnish famine causes about 15 percent of Finland's population to die in Europe's last major naturally caused famine.

1876–1878 In the Great Famine of India, over 5 million die of hunger or disease.

1919 The charity Save the Children is first established in the UK.

1921–1922 Famine in the Volga-Ural region of Russia kills 5 million people.

1932–1933 Food scarcity leads to famine in agricultural Russia (Ukraine). As many as 10 million starve to death.

1939–1945 World War II: victims starve in concentration camps in Nazi Germany.

1940–1943 Famine is deadly in the Warsaw Ghetto, Poland.

1942 The charity Oxfam is founded in the UK, originally as the Oxford Committee for Famine Relief.

1945 The Food and Agriculture Organization of the United Nations (FAO) is founded in Canada to lead international efforts to defeat hunger in both developing and developed countries.

1959–1961 20 million people perish in the Great Chinese Famine.

1963 The United Nations World Food Program (WFP) is founded.

1984–1985 8 million famine victims starve in Ethiopia; 1 million die.

1985 Live Aid concerts, organized by Bob Geldof, raise money for famine victims in Ethiopia.

1988 Nonprofit fair trade certification enables more customers to buy fair trade agricultural products and to track the origin of the goods.

2000–present Land reforms by President Mugabe cause a food crisis in Zimbabwe.

2003–present The Darfur conflict causes famine across Sudan.

2004 The Indian Ocean tsunami hits many countries, including Indonesia, Thailand, Sri Lanka, and Somalia, killing over 200,000 people.

2006 Food crisis threatens the Horn of Africa (Eritrea, Ethiopia, Djibouti, and Somalia).

2008 Burmese authorities obstruct foreign aid sent to relieve victims of Cyclone Nargis.

2008 Drought and hunger return to Ethiopia.

2008 Rocketing food prices hit developing countries particularly badly. There are riots in Haiti, Ethiopia, Senegal, and many other countries around the world.

2008 WFP celebrates its 45th anniversary. WFP has fed over 1.4 billion of the world's poorest people and invested more than $30 billion in development and emergency relief.

GLOSSARY

biofuel crops Crops including maize (corn) and soy that are grown to produce fuel, such as ethanol.

blight A plant disease often caused by a fungus or virus.

catastrophe A sudden disaster.

corrupt Dishonest.

democracy A form of government that gives people the right to vote for, or elect, its members.

developed world Wealthy nations like the United States, United Kingdom and most of Western Europe, with large industries and relatively high average income per member of the population.

developing world Nations seeking to build their industries and wealth, who tend to be poorer and contain many poor people.

drought A very long period of extremely dry weather, causing water shortages and crop failures.

economy The goods, services, and wealth produced by a society.

famine Drastic hunger or starvation due to long-term shortages of food.

genetically modified (GM) crops Edible plants that have been changed through genetic engineering—an artificial way of using science to produce better plants.

humanitarian Showing concern for others, doing things for charity, or to do with human rights.

infrastructure The basic facilities and services that help a society to work well. This usually includes transportation, factories, schools, and water and power lines.

malnutrition A lack of healthy food in the diet, causing weakness and other health problems.

nongovernmental organizations (NGOs) Organizations, such as charities, that are not part of local or state government.

refugee camp A place where people who have been forced to leave their homes go to live.

staple food The main type of food eaten, such as rice, wheat or potatoes.

Third World debt Now more commonly known as developing countries' debt. Many African countries owe large sums of money to developed countries.

tsunami A huge ocean wave, usually caused by an underwater earthquake.

United Nations (UN) An international organization with more than 190 member countries, which was formed in 1945 to promote world peace, good health, and economic development.

vulnerable Especially at risk.

World Food Program (WFP) The United Nations food aid agency.

RESOURCES

Books

Ethiopia (Cultures of the World)
by Steven Gish, Winnie Thay, and Zamiah Abdul Latif *Marshall Cavendish Benchmark*, 2007

Hungry Planet: What the World Eats
by Faith D'Aluisio, Photographs by Peter Menzel *Ten Speed Press*, 2007

Web Sites

http://www.fao.org/about/get-involved/en
The Food and Agriculture Organization of the United Nations shows different ways to get involved in ending world hunger, starting locally and expanding nationally. It also has a great page on World Food Day.

http://www.food-force.com
Download and play fun games to donate food on this web site! Managed by the World Food Organization, this web site also provides teacher's links with lesson plans on world hunger and how students can get involved through learning.

http://www.globalcitizencorps.org/issues.htm?page=issues_hunger
From the organization Global Citizens Corp, this web page breaks down world hunger and answers and explains common questions. The site also provides links to other worldwide problems, and links to other organizations concerned with ending world hunger.

http://www.wfp.org
The official site for the World Food Organization has lots of information about world hunger in the Hunger tab. The web site provides an interactive map, up-to-date statistics, and FAQ. There are also specific pages for students and teachers.

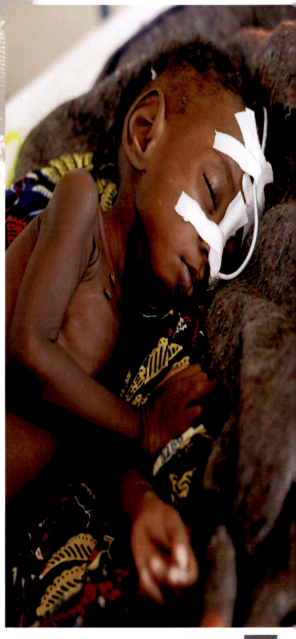

INDEX

Numbers in *italics* refer to captions.

Afghanistan 7, *7*
Africa 9, *9*, 10, 13, 24, 28, 29
aid 28, 29, 32, *32*, 33, *33*, 34, 35, *35*
Albania 41
Australia 20

Bangladesh 19, *19*, 26
Belarus *16*
Bell, Martin 12
biofuel crops 38
Burma 35, *35*

Canada 21
Chad *34*
charities 26–27, 30, 31, 32, 40
child deaths 7, *10*, 31
climate change 20
corruption 33

Darfur 12, *13*
democracy 18, 29
Democratic Republic of Congo 11
developed world 6, 32, 33, 36, 38
developing world 7, 22, 25, 28, 32, 33, 39, 41
droughts 9, 20, 40

education 18, 33, 41
Egypt 14
El Salvador *31*
Eritrea 10
Ethiopia 9, *9*

fair trade 24–25, *24*
famine 8–9, 11, 13, 14, 18, 37
flooding 9, 19, *19*, 34, *34*, 35, 40
food aid 18, 27, 34, 40–41, *40*
food price increases 38–39, *38*, 39
foreign aid 32–33, *33*, 34
free press 18

Geldof, Bob 28, *28*
genetically modified (GM) crops 22–23, *22*, *23*
Ghana 24, *24*
golden rice 22
governments 9, 18–19, 27

Haiti 39, *39*
health care 18, 24
hunger 6–7

India 13, *13*, *23*, 37
Indonesia 32, *32*
Irish Potato Famine 8, *8*

Live 8 concerts 28–29, *28*, *29*
livestock 21

Mali *41*
malnutrition 7, 10–11, *11*, 20, 22, *30*, 31
meat 21
Médecins Sans Frontières 30
media 12–13
Millennium Development Goal 31
Mugabe, President 27
Museveni, Yoweri 18
Myanmar 35, *35*

Nepal 11
news 30
Niger *30*, 31
nongovernmental organizations (NGOs) 26, 32, 40
North Korea 11
Norway 36
nutrients 10, 22
nutrition *41*
overeating 6

Pakistan 25, *25*
Palestine *40*
Philippines 22, *22*
poverty 14–15, 17, 28, 29, 41
press coverage 12–13

Red Cross *40*
refugees 12, *13*, 34, *34*
riots 39

Save the Children 31
schooling 14, 24
Somalia 17, *17*
Sri Lanka 40
starvation 8, 11, 13, 30, 37, 41
Sudan 12, *13*, 34, *34*
supermarkets *6*, 36, 38

Thailand *26*
Third World debt 28
Tibet *20*
transport 18
tsunami 32, *32*

Uganda 18, *18*
United Kingdom (U.K.) 28, 37
United Nations World Food Program 13, *31*, 32, *40*
United States 6, *6*, 15, *15*, 21, 33, 36, 37

violence 12, 17
vitamin A deficiency 22
Voluntary Service Overseas (VSO) *26*

war 9, 12, 34, *40*
wasting food 36–37
world population 7, 20

Zimbabwe 27, *27*